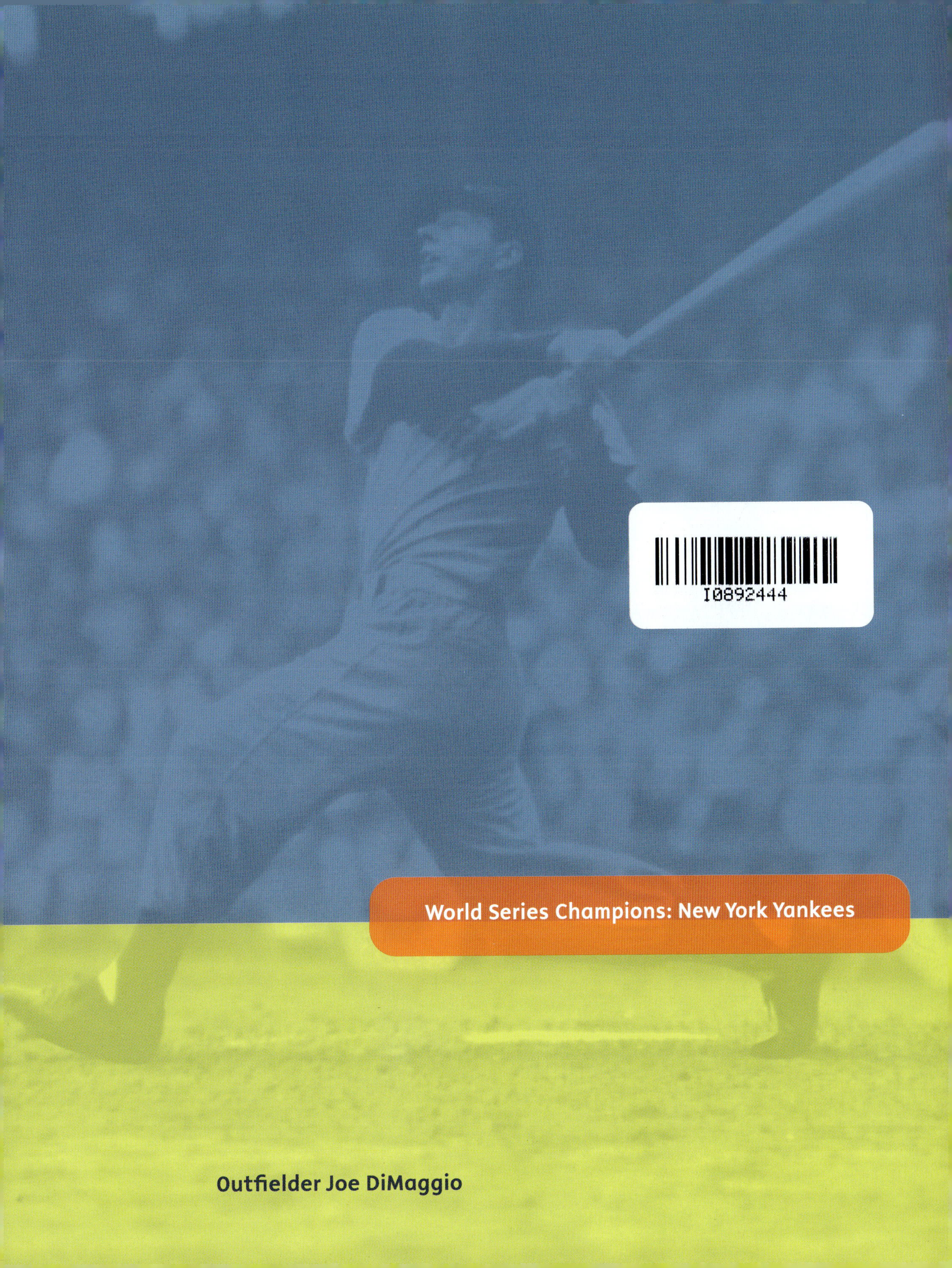

World Series Champions: New York Yankees

Outfielder Joe DiMaggio

Second baseman Gleyber Torres

WORLD SERIES CHAMPIONS

NEW YORK YANKEES

MICHAEL E. GOODMAN

CREATIVE EDUCATION / CREATIVE PAPERBACKS

Published by Creative Education and Creative Paperbacks
P.O. Box 227, Mankato, Minnesota 56002
Creative Education and Creative Paperbacks are imprints of
The Creative Company
www.thecreativecompany.us

Art Direction by Tom Morgan
Book production by Ciara Beitlich
Edited by Joe Tischler

Photographs by Alamy (Aflo Co. Ltd.), Corbis (Focus on Sport), Dreamstime (Songquan Deng), Getty (Diamond Images, Chris McGrath, Jim McIsaac, Rich Pilling, Vaughn Ridley, Robert Riger, Transcendental Graphics)

Library of Congress Cataloging-in-Publication Data
Names: Goodman, Michael E., author.
Title: New York Yankees / Michael E. Goodman.
Description: Mankato, MN : Creative Education and Creative Paperbacks, [2024] | Series: Creative sports: World Series champions | Includes index. | Audience: Ages 7-10 | Audience: Grades 2-3 | Summary: "Elementary-level text and engaging sports photos highlight the New York Yankees' MLB World Series wins and losses, plus sensational players associated with the professional baseball team such as Aaron Judge."-- Provided by publisher.
Identifiers: LCCN 2023008228 (print) | LCCN 2023008229 (ebook) | ISBN 9781640268302 (library binding) | ISBN 9781682773802 (paperback) | ISBN 9781640269835 (pdf)
Subjects: LCSH: New York Yankees (Baseball team)--History--Juvenile literature. | Baseball players--New York (State)--New York--History--Juvenile literature. | Baseball--New York (State)--New York--History--Juvenile literature.
Classification: LCC GV875.N4 G67 2024 (print) | LCC GV875.N4 (ebook) | DDC 796.357/64097471--dc23/eng/20230302
LC record available at https://lccn.loc.gov/2023008228
LC ebook record available at https://lccn.loc.gov/2023008229

Printed in China

2009 World Series Champions

Pitcher Gerrit Cole

CONTENTS

Home of the Yankees

New York is the largest city in the United States. Close to nine million people live there. Many are baseball fans who love the Yankees. They pack Yankee **Stadium** to watch their team play.

The New York Yankees are the most successful team in Major League Baseball (MLB) history. They are part of the American League (AL) East Division. Their biggest **rivals** are the Boston Red Sox. All MLB teams try to win the World Series to become champions. The Yankees have won 27 World Series **titles**!

Outfielder Mickey Mantle

Naming the Yankees

The team's first home field was on a high hill. So, the players were called the Highlanders. Sportswriters thought that name was too long to use in their stories. They called the club the Yankees, or Yanks, instead. In 1913, team owners officially changed the name.

Outfielder Babe Ruth

Yankees History

New York played its first season in 1903. Up-and-down years followed. The team's luck changed in 1920. Hard-hitting outfielder Babe Ruth arrived in a deal with the Boston Red Sox. He immediately began setting home run records. Ruth powered the Yankees to three World Series titles during the 1920s.

The Yankees won five more championships in the 1930s. First baseman Lou Gehrig played in every game for 13 seasons in a row. Outfielder Joe DiMaggio was a star at bat and in the field. Later, outfielder Mickey Mantle and catcher Yogi Berra lifted the team even higher. They helped the Yankees win five straight World Series from 1949 to 1953. By 1962, New York had 20 trophies!

The Yankees went into a **slump** after that. They finally won two more titles in 1977 and 1978. Slugging outfielder Reggie Jackson led the way.

Catcher Yogi Berra

Shortstop Derek Jeter

Then, starting in 1995, the Yanks reached the **playoffs** for 13 straight years. Joe Torre was the manager for 12 of those years. The team also won four more titles.

The Yankees have had a winning record every season in the 2000s. The team captain many of those years was shortstop Derek Jeter. He smashed more than 3,400 hits during his Yankees career. Ace relief pitcher Mariano Rivera saved 652 games. That's most in baseball history.

Other Yankees Stars

The Yankees have had many All-Star pitchers. Whitey Ford was a big winner in the 1950s. Ron Guidry starred in the 1970s. C. C. Sabathia was great in the 2010s.

First baseman Don Mattingly won awards for his hitting and fielding. Yankees fans called him "Donnie Baseball."

First baseman Don Mattingly

Outfielder Aaron Judge

Outfielder Aaron Judge belted 62 home runs in 2022. Fans are hoping he can help the Yankees become champions again soon!

WORLD SERIES CHAMPIONS

Glossary

playoffs—games that the best teams play after a regular season to see who the champion will be

rival—a team that plays extra hard against another team

slump—a period of time when a team loses more games than it wins

stadium—a building with tiers of seats for spectators

title—another word for championship

About the Yankees

Started playing: 1903

League/division: American League, East Division

Team colors: navy blue and white

Home stadium: Yankee Stadium

New York Yankees website: www.mlb.com/yankees

WORLD SERIES CHAMPIONSHIPS:

1923, 4 games to 2 over New York Giants
1927, 4 games to 0 over Pittsburgh Pirates
1928, 4 games to 0 over St. Louis Cardinals
1932, 4 games to 0 over Chicago Cubs
1936, 4 games to 2 over New York Giants
1937, 4 games to 1 over New York Giants
1938, 4 games to 0 over Chicago Cubs
1939, 4 games to 0 over Cincinnati Reds
1941, 4 games to 1 over Brooklyn Dodgers
1943, 4 games to 1 over St. Louis Cardinals
1947, 4 games to 3 over Brooklyn Dodgers
1949, 4 games to 1 over Brooklyn Dodgers
1950, 4 games to 0 over Philadelphia Phillies
1951, 4 games to 2 over New York Giants
1952, 4 games to 3 over Brooklyn Dodgers
1953, 4 games to 2 over Brooklyn Dodgers
1956, 4 games to 3 over Brooklyn Dodgers
1958, 4 games to 3 over Milwaukee Braves
1961, 4 games to 1 over Cincinnati Reds
1962, 4 games to 3 over San Francisco Giants
1977, 4 games to 2 over Los Angeles Dodgers
1978, 4 games to 2 over Los Angeles Dodgers
1996, 4 games to 2 over Atlanta Braves
1998, 4 games to 0 over San Diego Padres
1999, 4 games to 0 over Atlanta Braves
2000, 4 games to 1 over New York Mets
2009, 4 games to 2 over Philadelphia Phillies

Outfielder Reggie Jackson

Index